Peter Stuyvesant

Dutch Military Leader

Colonial Leaders

Lord Baltimore *English Politician and Colonist*

Benjamin Banneker *American Mathematician and Astronomer*

William Bradford *Governor of Plymouth Colony*

Benjamin Franklin *American Statesman, Scientist, and Writer*

Anne Hutchinson *Religious Leader*

Cotton Mather *Author, Clergyman, and Scholar*

William Penn *Founder of Democracy*

John Smith *English Explorer and Colonist*

Miles Standish *Plymouth Colony Leader*

Peter Stuyvesant *Dutch Military Leader*

Revolutionary War Leaders

Benedict Arnold *Traitor to the Cause*

Nathan Hale *Revolutionary Hero*

Alexander Hamilton *First U.S. Secretary of the Treasury*

Patrick Henry *American Statesman and Speaker*

Thomas Jefferson *Author of the Declaration of Independence*

John Paul Jones *Father of the U.S. Navy*

Thomas Paine *Political Writer*

Paul Revere *American Patriot*

Betsy Ross *American Patriot*

George Washington *First U.S. President*

Peter Stuyvesant

Dutch Military Leader

Joan Banks

Arthur M. Schlesinger, jr.
Senior Consulting Editor

Chelsea House Publishers

Philadelphia

Produced by Robert Gerson Publisher's Services, Avondale, PA

CHELSEA HOUSE PUBLISHERS
Editor in Chief Stephen Reginald
Production Manager Pamela Loos
Director of Photography Judy L. Hasday
Art Director Sara Davis
Managing Editor James D. Gallagher

Staff for *PETER STUYVESANT*
Project Editor Anne Hill
Project Editor/Publishing Coordinator Jim McAvoy
Contributing Editor Amy Handy
Associate Art Director Takeshi Takahashi
Series Design Keith Trego

The Chelsea House World Wide Web address is http://www.chelseahouse.com

First Printing
1 3 5 7 9 8 6 4 2

Library of Congress Cataloging-in-Publication Data

Banks, Joan
Peter Stuyvesant / by Joan Banks.
    p. cm. — (Colonial leaders)
Includes bibliographical references and index.
Summary: A biography of the hot-tempered leader who, though intolerant and
unpopular, brought major reforms to the colony of New Netherlands before its
surrender to the British in 1664.
ISBN 0–7910–5346–6 (hc);   0–7910–5689–9 (pb)
1. Stuyvesant, Peter, 1592–1672 Juvenile literature 2. Governors—New York
(State)—Biography Juvenile literature. 3. New York (State)—History——Colonial
period, ca. 1600–1775 Biography Juvenile literature. 4. New Netherland
Biography Juvenile literature. [1. Stuyvesant, Peter , 1592–1672. 2. Governors.
3. New York (N.Y.)—History—Colonial period, ca. 1600-1775.] I. Title. II. Series
F122.1.S78B36 1999
974.7'02'092—dc21
[B]   99–24901
                                                                       CIP

The author wishes to thank Charles Gehring, head of the New Netherland Project
at the New York State Library, for his help in researching this work.

> **Publisher's Note:** In Colonial and Revolutionary War America, there were no standard rules for spelling, punctuation, capitalization, or grammar. Some of the quotations that appear in the Colonial Leaders and Revolutionary War Leaders series come from original documents and letters written during this time in history. Original quotations reflect writing inconsistencies of the period.

Contents

Peter Stuyvesant grew up in the Netherlands, a land still famous for its tulips and also known for its many windmills. These structures use the power of the wind to create energy and keep the low-lying country safe from the sea.

Stubborn Pete

Mrs. Stuyvesant rocked the wooden cradle to quiet the crying baby. The baby was her son, Peter. He was already headstrong. She didn't know his temper would become famous. Some people would even call him "Stubborn Pete" behind his back.

His name, Peter Stuyvesant, became famous, too. He was the last governor of New Netherland. Today the area covers parts of New York, New Jersey, Delaware, and Connecticut.

New Netherland was named after a country in Europe called the Netherlands, which is also known as Holland. The people who live there are called the

Dutch. And that was where Peter Stuyvesant was born, in 1610 or 1611. (No one is sure exactly when.)

"Netherlands" means lowlands. Much of the land lies below sea level. The people built **dikes** to hold back the sea. As a child, Peter ran and played along the dikes. He passed gardens filled with tulips. The Netherlands is still famous for its tulips.

Peter stopped and watched the huge arms of windmills turning in the wind. The windmills helped keep the lowlands safe from the sea. They pumped ground water and rain water over the dikes and into **canals**. The canals carried the water to the sea. In the winter the canals froze, and the children skated on them.

From time to time a dike would break. Peter and his sister, Anna, and their parents joined the neighbors and worked together to repair it. Even people who were quarreling stopped to help each other. They made "dike peace."

Peter's father was a minister. He hoped Peter would be a minister too, so he sent his son to

In Holland today, modern machinery is used to control water levels, but in Stuyvesant's time a system of dikes and canals did the job.

the University of Franeker. But Peter didn't want to be a minister. He wanted more excitement in his life.

He went to Amsterdam, the capital of the Netherlands, to get a job. He found one with the Dutch West India Company. This company was very powerful. The Dutch government gave it control over all Dutch trade with western Africa and North and South America. It had colonies in many places.

The company sent Peter to a small island east of Brazil. For the first time he got to travel across the sea. It was exciting for the young man from the lowlands to see new plants, colorful birds, and other strange animals in the **tropics**. Palm trees lined sandy beaches, and the weather was very hot and wet.

Peter worked hard, and before long the company gave him a new job on the island of Curaçao in the **West Indies**. Peter settled into his work. He ran Curaçao and several other nearby islands for the company. He shipped salt, wood for yellow dye, and horses back to the Netherlands. But day-to-day life was not very exciting in Curaçao.

Then one day he received an order from the Dutch West India Company. He was to take the island of St. Martin away from the Spanish. St. Martin was about 500 miles north of Curaçao.

He thought taking the island would be easy because he had heard that St. Martin had few soldiers in its fort. But his information was wrong. The Spanish had many soldiers waiting at St. Martin.

With seven ships and about 300 men, Peter sailed to the island. When they arrived, they threw up a low wall facing the fort. They mounted cannon on the wall. Then Peter climbed onto the wall to put up the Dutch flag.

The Spanish fired. A cannonball hit Peter in the right leg. He was badly hurt and was out of the fight before it began. He was taken to another island, where doctors removed his leg.

Peter went to work on the island of Curaçao, where he was in charge of shipping various goods back to his company in the Netherlands.

His men continued to fight for a month. They wanted to take the fort. But more Spanish soldiers arrived. The Dutch were outnumbered and had to give up.

Peter was very disappointed. He didn't like to fail.

Back in Curaçao, Peter tried to work, but he was ill. The stump of his leg did not get well. That summer he asked the company to let him return to Holland. He thought doctors there might help him.

The company agreed, and Peter sailed back to the Netherlands in the fall of 1644 to recover from his injury. While he was there, he was fitted with a peg leg. It had bands of silver around it. Later, some people called him "Old Silver Leg." Like "Stubborn Pete," it was another nickname people used behind his back.

A well-known statue in New York City depicts Peter Stuyvesant striking a commanding pose and surveying the square named in his honor.

2

A New
Job

Peter limped through his sister's house on his new peg leg. He was restless. He wanted to get back to work.

He was staying with Anna, her husband, Samuel Bayard, and their children while he got used to his new leg. They lived in a town near the city of Rotterdam in the Netherlands.

Peter worried that the Dutch West India Company was unhappy with him. After all, his attack on St. Martin had been a failure. But the company thought Peter had done all he could. The directors were pleased with him. Peter was glad to hear it, and he asked them to put him back to work.

The company had big plans for him. It needed someone who was a strong leader and a hard worker to head its **colony** in North America. Peter was just such a man.

In May 1645 the company appointed him to be the governor of New Netherland. He was also asked to continue as governor of Curaçao and the nearby islands of Bonaire and Aruba. It would be quite a job. Now Peter had to wait until the Dutch government approved his appointment.

While he waited, he learned all he could about the colony where he was going. New Netherland was founded 21 years earlier, in 1624. The Dutch West India Company had sent 30 families to settle along what is now called the Hudson River in North America. Some of the people built Fort Orange at a site near present-day Albany, New York. It was the first permanent white settlement in New Netherland. The company was eager for these colonists to start trading with the Native Americans. It especially wanted beaver furs to sell in Europe.

Colonists traded many items with the Indians, such as the dishes and jewelry seen here. They especially wanted furs to send back to Europe.

The following year, more colonists arrived. Some of them built a fort at the foot of what is now called Manhattan. They named it Fort Amsterdam, after the capital of the Netherlands. The village that grew up around the fort was named New Amsterdam.

A governor was sent to the new colony in 1626. He worried that there would be trouble with the Native Americans. Fights might break out over who owned Manhattan Island. To be safe, he decided to buy the land.

He met with some Indians in the area and traded tools, trinkets, and beads for the land. The Indians didn't understand the idea of buying and selling land. They didn't believe land was something to own. But they took the tools, trinkets, and beads the governor offered.

Some people say what he gave them was worth about $24. Others say it was more like $2,000. In either case, it was a good deal. Today the island is worth billions.

While Peter was waiting to be sent to New Netherland, he met Samuel Bayard's sister, Judith. The two fell in love, and he asked Judith to marry him. They married in August 1645 in a little church in Breda in the Netherlands. It was the very church where Judith had been baptized in 1608.

Finally the government gave its okay, and Peter took the oath of office in July 1646. It had

One of the most famous trades of all time was the exchange of some trinkets and tools with the Indians in return for the island of Manhattan.

been over a year since the Dutch West India Company had appointed him.

On Christmas Day Peter and Judith boarded a ship that would take them to New Netherland. They were leaving the Old World for the New.

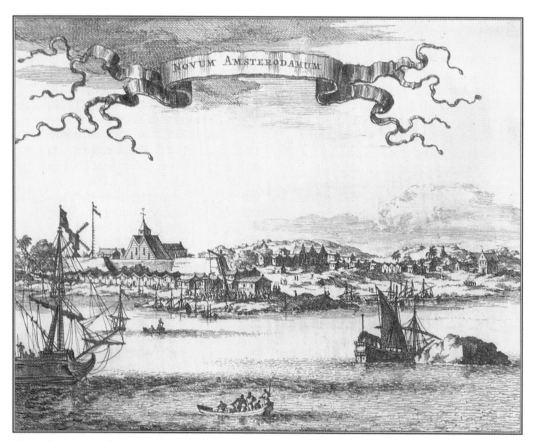

At the southern tip of the island arose the village of New Amsterdam. A scene like this greeted Peter's arrival in the colony.

Four ships sailed together. Most of the passengers were soldiers. Some were families who were going to settle in the New World.

Peter ordered the ships to sail first to Curaçao. Maybe he wanted to show the island to his new wife. It might have been her only chance to see the tropics. He probably also wanted to see how things were going. After all, he was in charge of Curaçao.

But the West Indies was out of the way, and the trip was rough. The voyage took more than four months. The ships finally sailed into New Amsterdam on May 11, 1647.

Peter and Judith stepped out on the deck of the ship and took their first look at their new home. A cluster of buildings and houses lined the shore. A Dutch flag atop the fort blew in the breeze. Towering above the fort were the blades of a windmill. Peter noticed that it was too close to the fort to catch the wind very well, but even so, the windmill made the town look like home.

Peter was a strict governor who thought he had to be firm with rules to do his job well, and "Stubborn Pete" also had a short temper. Many of the people wanted more say in the government.

Getting Down
to Business

1t didn't take long for the news to spread in the tiny village of about 700 people: a ship had arrived. Many of the **burghers**, or citizens, left what they were doing. They hurried down to take a look at their new governor. They lined the bank as Peter and Judith were rowed ashore.

The ex-governor paraded Peter through the streets, which were more like cow paths. They were unpaved and muddy, and lined with trash. How they smelled!

Peter noticed the garbage. People seemed to throw it out their doors right onto the unpaved roads. Pigs and chickens were running loose everywhere, and the pigs rooted through the garbage.

Peter noticed the roofs on the houses. They were made of **thatch**. Smoke curled from wooden chimneys. What a fire hazard!

New Amsterdam was a smelly, dirty, unsafe town.

The burghers showed Peter the fort. He saw that some of its walls were falling apart. He had heard about the terrible Indian wars in New Netherland. What good would this falling-down fort do if there was another attack?

Peter knew he had much to do.

While Peter was looking over the town on that first day, the people were looking over this tall stranger. He wore his hair shoulder length in the style of the time. His forehead was wide, and his nose was long. They noticed his fine hat with its plume. They noticed the sword that hung from his waist. And they noticed one more thing: his silver-banded peg leg.

They greeted their new governor as he passed. They hadn't liked the old governor.

They wondered if they would like this new one any better. Some of them thought he strutted like a peacock.

He gave a speech at the fort. "I shall be as a father over his children," he told the people.

The people weren't sure they needed a father. They wanted more say in the government. But Peter knew his job. The Dutch West India Company wanted him to make money for the company. To do so, he thought he needed to be firm like a father. He wanted the people to know he was boss.

The ex-governor, who name was Kieft, made a speech at the fort, too. Some of the people yelled angrily at him. Peter knew there had been trouble between Kieft and the burghers. Now he saw it for himself.

Peter set to work. He told the people what they could and could not do. He closed the taverns at nine o'clock every evening. He fined people for fighting in the streets. He said that pigs must be kept behind fences, and that

outhouses must be removed from the streets.

Walking along the streets of New Amsterdam was dangerous because people drove their carts and horses too fast. Peter made a new law. He said the drivers must get down from their carts and lead their horses. They could only ride through town on the street now called Broadway. Even on Broadway, he set a speed limit.

Peter was a religious man. He believed Sunday was for going to church. People were no longer allowed to work on Sunday. If they did so, they were fined. He ordered two services on Sunday instead of one.

Thatched roofs and wooden chimneys were banned. Haystacks near houses had to be removed. He appointed fire wardens. They went from house to house and fined people whose houses were fire traps.

The Dutch West India Company's main business was fur trading. The company put a tax on every fur taken from the colony. Some people were smuggling furs out of New Netherland

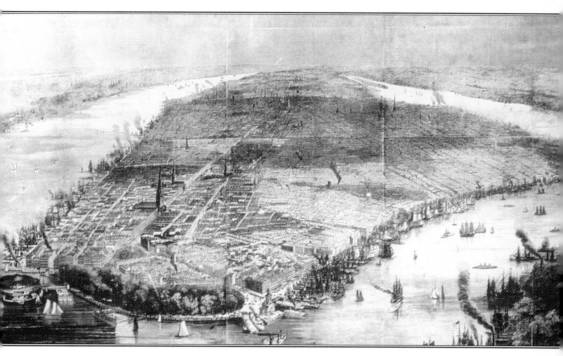

The settlement gradually spread over the island. Broadway, the wide street running diagonally uptown, is still a main thoroughfare today.

without paying the tax to the company. Peter set up a checkpoint on the river. All ships had to stop there to make sure they weren't smuggling out furs or other goods without paying the taxes.

There were new taxes. Peter hoped to repair the church and the fort with some of the tax money.

He appointed a **council** of nine men from the town to give him advice. He also asked for money to repair the fort. The Council of Nine said no. They said the Dutch West India Company should pay to repair the fort.

In the 1600s, people loved beaver hats. Beavers in Europe had been wiped out, so trappers looked for a new supply. They found it in North America. Native Americans trapped the beavers. They traded the pelts for tools and guns. The pelts were shipped to Europe to make into hats.

The Dutch West India Company didn't send the money. So Peter told the men of New Amsterdam they must do the job. He said each man must spend 12 days a year working on the fort or pay a fine. It was a good idea, but the men knew how to get out of the work. The fort didn't get repaired.

Before Peter had been in New Amsterdam two months, two burghers came to see him. The burghers, named Melyn and Kuyter, complained about the former governor. They said he had lied to the Dutch West India Company. They said he had caused the trouble with the

Indians. They wanted Peter to bring charges against Kieft.

Peter didn't like the two burghers telling him what to do. He believed a governor was a ruler who could do no wrong. A governor's word must be obeyed. He didn't like what the two burghers were saying about Kieft either.

Kieft was a clever man. He knew how Peter felt. So he complained about Melyn and Kuyter to Peter. He said the two men were wrong and that they had caused the troubles.

Peter believed Kieft. He had Melyn and Kuyter arrested. He called them troublemakers. He fined them and told them they must leave New Netherland forever. Melyn and Kuyter said they would go to Holland and **appeal** to the Dutch government.

The very idea made Peter boiling mad. He was said to have told Melyn that he would be "hung immediately on the highest tree in New Netherland" if he appealed. Peter's temper came out again in a meeting. He said that if anyone even thought about appealing to the Dutch government, he would "make him a foot shorter and send the pieces to Holland, and let him appeal in that way." His words just made Melyn and Kuyter more sure of what they should do.

The two burghers sailed for Holland in August 1647. Ex-governor Kieft sailed on the same ship. Before it reached Holland, a terrible storm arose. The ship broke apart, and 81 people were lost. Kieft was among them. Melyn and Kuyter were rescued. They went on to Holland to appeal their case. They later said that just before Kieft was lost in the sea, he had come to them and said, "Friends, I have done wrong. Can you forgive me?"

In New Amsterdam the Council of Nine was causing headaches for Peter. The council didn't want to be a Dutch West India Company colony. Council members believed the company was more interested in money than in the good of the colony. The people the company sent to settle New Netherland were often single men who didn't plan to stay there. If the colony was to succeed, the council said, it needed more families.

The council members also wanted more say in the way the town was run. They didn't want Peter to be their only boss. They'd had enough of that under Governor Kieft.

Peter agreed with the council members about some things, but he refused to let them call a public meeting. So they went door to door and talked to the citizens. One man named Adriaen van der Donck wrote down what the people said. He prepared a paper to take to the government in Holland.

By now many burghers were mad at Peter. They saw him as an enemy instead of a man who was doing his job for the company. Van der Donck's paper said Peter was a bad governor.

When Peter heard about the paper, he entered Van der Donck's rooms when he wasn't there. Peter took the paper and had Van der Donck arrested.

Adriaen van der Donck spoke for the people of New Amsterdam, who believed Peter should give them more of a chance to take part in government.

Meanwhile, Melyn, one of the burghers who had survived the shipwreck, came back to New Amsterdam. He had been to the Netherlands and made his appeal. Now he had an important letter from the Dutch government. He waited for just the right time to read the letter to the people of New Amsterdam. He wanted to embarrass Peter.

Soon that time came. Peter called a meeting of the citizens at the church. He wanted to talk about the state of the colony. People came from far and wide.

Melyn came to the meeting. He gave the letter from the Dutch government to another burgher, who stood up to read it. Peter got mad. He grabbed the letter. The two men had a tug-of-war over it.

Peter knew better than to act that way, but sometimes his temper took over. Now he backed off and let the man read the letter.

The letter said Melyn and Kuyter were right about the ex-governor. He had been a bad governor. He had been careless with the money of the Dutch West India Company and had caused the terrible Indian wars. Settlers and Native Americans had been killed, and many colonists had lost their homes and farms because of him.

The letter went on to say that Peter had treated the two burghers unfairly. It said they were no longer banned from living in New Netherland.

Peter had been trying to do what the Dutch West India Company wanted him to do. It wanted him to be a strong leader. It wanted him to make rules and see that the people followed the rules. The company didn't want the people to run things.

But the Dutch government didn't see things that way at all. It ordered Peter or his **representative** to come to Holland to defend his actions. Peter sent his secretary as his representative.

The Council of Nine let Van der Donck out of prison, and in August 1649 he left for Holland

The Dutch had come to the New World as traders, and the colony became a thriving port where many people conducted business. Ships brought goods back and forth across the ocean.

on the same ship as Peter's representative. Van der Donck was going to plead the case of the people of New Amsterdam.

In the Middle of Things

Not all of the colonists who came to America did so for the same reasons. The Dutch first came to the New World as traders. Their colony was New Netherland.

The English came mainly to settle and farm. They lived in New England, Maryland, and Virginia, colonies to the north and south of New Netherland. New Netherland was sandwiched in between.

The colonists were suspicious of one another. The English worried that the Native Americans were getting guns from Dutch traders. In fact the Dutch did trade guns to the Indians to keep peace with them.

The Dutch worried that the English settlers were taking Dutch land. In fact English people did live on what New Netherland considered to be its land.

But just what was Dutch land? What was English? The boundaries weren't clear. Peter wanted maps drawn up. He wanted the leaders to agree about the boundaries of their colonies. He thought that would help keep peace.

So in 1650 he called a meeting of New England leaders. The meeting was held in Hartford, in what is today Connecticut. The leaders were all there, but where was *there?* Was Hartford in New Netherland?

Peter thought so. But when he said so, the New England leaders got mad. Finally he agreed not to call it New Netherland. And the meeting went on.

Before the meeting was over, Peter had agreed that the English could have the eastern part of Long Island. Many English people lived there already. He also lost Hartford to

A Dutch family gathers around the fireplace in a New Amsterdam household. Since there was no electricity or central heating, they relied on large fireplaces for heat, light, and cooking.

the English. Giving up this land gave people in New Netherland another reason to be unhappy with Peter.

What he kept was the land along the Hudson River. The Dutch called it the North River.

Peter knew this land was more important to the Dutch West India Company than eastern Long Island. Traders used the river to bring their furs to New Amsterdam. Peter believed he had done the right thing. He was doing his job for the company.

Peter was happy about the **Treaty** of Hartford for another reason. When the English leaders signed the agreement, they were admitting that the Dutch had a claim to land in North America. Years later, though, Peter would learn that the treaty meant little to the English.

The English language borrowed many Dutch words, including *cookie*, *waffle*, *coleslaw*, *yacht*, *spook*, and *boss*. The name *Brooklyn* came from a Dutch word meaning "broken land." Other New York place names, like *Yonkers*, *Coney Island*, and *Harlem*, sprang from Dutch beginnings.

While Peter worried about boundaries, Adriaen van der Donck had been in Holland, trying to get more rights for the people of New Netherland. Finally the Dutch government listened. In 1652 it sent bad news to the colony: the Dutch West India Company was still in charge.

But there was good news for the people, too. Peter would no longer be the only leader of New Amsterdam. The Dutch government said the people could have a city council. They could elect two mayors, five **aldermen**, and a sheriff.

The burghers were thrilled. But Peter wasn't. He didn't want to share his power. So Stubborn Pete did it his way. Instead of letting the people *elect* the city council, he appointed it. It was not until 1658 that he finally let the people have an election. Even then, he still controlled things by letting them elect 16 people. From those, he chose the eight members of the city council. He didn't give up easily!

An order also came for Peter to sail to Holland to explain himself. This time the government didn't say he could send a representative. They wanted Peter himself. The government wanted to know why the people were complaining and why he had given up part of the colony.

But before he could go, England declared war on Holland. The government changed its mind. They told him to stay where he was. In wartime, New Netherland needed a strong leader, and Peter was that. He needed to protect New Netherland from the English colonies.

Peter Stuyvesant was at his best in a crisis. He now asked the people to work together to build a wall to protect the town. He asked them for money to pay for it, too. Work on the wall began. For a while quarrels were forgotten. It probably reminded Peter of the "dike peace" of his childhood.

They built the wall of wood. It was called a **palisade**. It stood twelve feet high. Inside it had a sloping platform. The guards could stand on the platform and look over the top of the wall. They could watch for enemies.

Word came that English warships had come into Boston harbor in New England. They were preparing to attack New Netherland.

Dutch soldiers patrolled along the palisade. They walked back and forth so many times, they wore a path. Later the path became known as

Today the home of the New York Stock Exchange, Wall Street once served as a northern boundary of the settlement, where the Dutch built a wall to defend themselves against the English.

Wall Street. It still lies at the lower end of Manhattan in New York City. Wall Street was the north boundary of New Amsterdam.

Luckily, the attack never came. Instead, England and Holland made peace.

With the war over, Peter sailed to the West Indies. He visited other Dutch colonies. He wanted more trading between the new city and the colonies in the Caribbean Sea.

When he returned, he was met by a Dutch ship in the New Amsterdam harbor. It brought word that the Dutch West India Company wanted him to capture New Sweden, a colony along the South River, now called the Delaware River.

Some years earlier, before Peter came to New Netherland, people from Sweden had set up a colony in part of New Netherland. They had named it New Sweden.

In 1651 Peter built Fort Casimir on the South River to take back some of the land. Once the fort was built, though, the Dutch did not take care of it. The Swedes captured Fort Casimir in 1654. They built another fort up the South River and called it Christina, after the Swedish queen.

The two Swedish forts blocked the fur trade coming down the river. Now the Dutch West India Company wanted the Swedes to leave.

Peter raised an army of more than 300 soldiers and a company of sailors. In seven ships, they sailed off to war.

They came to Fort Casimir first. The troops landed. Then, before a single shot was fired, the fort **surrendered.**

The Dutch soldiers grumbled. Some war!

Peter and his ships sailed on up the river to Fort Christina. The governor of New Sweden himself was there.

Peter sent a message to the governor. It told him to give up the fort and all of the South River. Peter waited for an answer.

While he waited, his soldiers had little to do. So they went into the countryside and killed cows, pigs, chickens, and goats. They robbed houses and fought with the settlers of New Sweden.

The soldiers in Fort Christina couldn't help the settlers. There were only about 30 of them, and they had little ammunition. All they could do was wish that Peter Stuyvesant and his army would go away.

A messenger took another letter from Peter to the governor in the fort. It told the Swedes to surrender the fort within 24 hours, or else.

The governor of New Sweden knew his men didn't have a chance. He surrendered. No human lives were lost. The South River was now back in the hands of the Dutch.

While the Dutch were waiting for the Swedes to give up, they received a message from New Amsterdam. Indians were on the attack. They had murdered settlers and burned down many houses.

Peter read the message with alarm. Was his family safe? He didn't just have his wife to think of. He now had two sons, Balthazar and Nicholas. His sister, Anna, now a widow, and her children had come to New Amsterdam, too.

The message continued. It said his family was safe in the fort.

As soon as New Sweden surrendered, Peter and his army hurried back to New Amsterdam. In those days it took a long time for messages to be sent. Days and days had passed since Peter had received word about the Indian attack. What would he find when he got back?

When the ships arrived, Peter saw the burned houses. People were crowded into the fort. He asked what had caused the Native Americans to attack.

Canoes loaded with hundreds of Indians had set out to attack an enemy tribe on Long Island. Some of them had come ashore for food near New Amsterdam. They wandered into the town and into homes. A few came onto the land of a man named Hendrick van Dyck.

Van Dyck didn't like Indians. He had fought them when Kieft was governor. When he saw an Indian woman picking peaches from his trees, he took out his gun and shot her. Within 24 hours, the Native Americans had killed Van Dyck.

People were scared. Many hurried into the fort for safety. Outside the fort, burning and killing began. Before it was over, at least 50 colonists and 60 Indians had been killed. Many settlers had been taken captive and 28 farms had been destroyed.

This was one time when Peter wasn't head-strong. He thought about his plans carefully. He didn't want to start a long Indian war like ex-governor Kieft. His most important job was to get the captive settlers back. He met with the Indian leaders and was able to buy the freedom of most of the captives. The Indians held others for up to two years.

Peter also ordered the settlers to live in villages for their own safety. If they chose not to, they were fined. The first settlement in New Jersey was founded as a result of Peter's order. It was called Bergen. The people built a palisade around it. They lived inside the walls and they had their gardens and farms outside. During the day they drove their cattle outside. At night they brought them back inside and closed the gates.

War with the Native Americans came again in 1659. No one knows what started this war, but it lasted for about nine months. Peter visited the Indians and made peace by making promises and bringing gifts to them. The Indians warned him there would be more trouble because a new town was being built on land they farmed.

In 1663 the Indians attacked the new town. But the colonists struck back again and again. The Native Americans lost their use of the land and many of their people before the war ended in 1664.

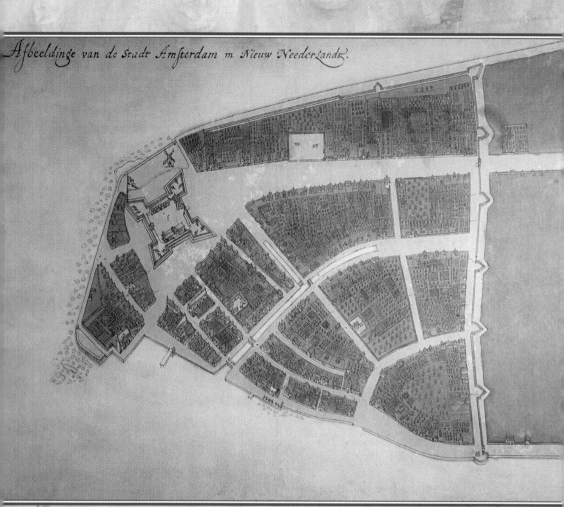

Afbeeldinge van de Stadt Amsterdam in Nieuw Neederlandt.

A map from Peter's time clearly shows the layout of New Amsterdam, with its streets, farms, and fort, and to protect it all, the palisade built along what would become Wall Street.

The Good and the Bad

Between the outbreaks of trouble, ordinary life in New Netherland went on. Unlike the ex-governor Kieft, Peter traveled through his colony. He had been up the North River to Fort Orange. He had traveled to Hartford on the Connecticut River. He had been along the South River and to what is now New Jersey. He saw the mountains and the rivers and the forests of this new world. He had grown up in the old country where the land was crowded. In New Netherland, most of the land was wilderness.

In all of New Netherland, only New Amsterdam had a large number of people. By 1660 about 1500 citizens and 342 houses made up the city. Many new colonists came to live there. The city did its business in the town hall, a former tavern that the city bought from the Dutch West India Company in 1654.

Many of the houses in New Amsterdam were brick and had tall roofs. They often had Dutch doors, a type of door with two halves. On nice days people stood with the top half of the door open and talked to people passing by. The lower half was closed to keep out dogs and chickens.

An old woman asked a New Netherland baker for a dozen cookies. He counted out 12. "One more than 12 makes a dozen," she said. He refused to give her another cookie. He began to have bad luck. She returned and asked for a dozen cookies. He counted out 13. Today "a baker's dozen" means 13.

Other people sat on their **stoops**, or porches. Outhouses no longer lined the streets. Little gardens grew by the houses.

The port was busy. Peter had a larger dock built, and ships came from all over the world. Ships from New England carried beef, wheat, apples, iron, and tar. From Virginia came tobacco. And down the North River came beaver and other pelts. In January 1660 about 30,000 animal pelts were shipped down the river from Fort Orange. The ships stopped at New Amsterdam and paid taxes to the Dutch West India Company. Taxes were the price of doing business in New Netherland.

While Peter was governor, the town gained a hospital and a post office. There was a home for orphans and another for the poor.

Peter set up the first fire department in America. Every house paid a tax of one beaver pelt. The tax went for leather buckets to carry water to put out fires. A shoemaker made the buckets. The money also bought ladders and hooks.

When there was a fire, people came running. Each person brought his leather bucket. They formed two lines. The buckets were filled at a spring or a pump or from the canal that ran through the town. Then the buckets were passed down the line. The last person tossed the water on the fire. The empty buckets were passed down the other line and refilled. This was known as a bucket **brigade**.

Peter started a night watch, or rattle watch. Four men walked through New Amsterdam after dark. They watched for signs of fire. They also looked for anyone up to no good. Each watchman carried a rattle that he shook as he walked. The sound let the people know someone was looking out for them.

When Peter and his family first came to New Amsterdam, they lived in a house inside the fort. Later they moved to a new house at the tip of Manhattan Island. It was called the "Great House." The house was made of very light gray stone, so light that it was later called the "White Hall." The street where it stood is now called Whitehall Street. The governor and his wife entertained there. Gardens grew to the water's edge, and Peter had a boat docked nearby.

In town Peter usually traveled on foot. Often four bodyguards went along with him. He also

Peter and his family moved into White Hall, a large, light gray stone house at the very tip of Manhattan surrounded by a beautiful garden.

had a carriage that was drawn by two horses.

Peter bought a **bowery**, or farm, outside of New Amsterdam from the Dutch West India Company. It was north of the city wall in what is now called the Bowery in New York City. A small village grew up around his farm. Peter had

Peter was very religious, and he built a chapel on his bowery. When he died many years later, he was buried there. More than 120 years after that, this church, St. Mark's-in-the-Bowery, was built on the spot and stands today.

a schoolmaster come to the village to teach the local children, although his own boys had a private tutor.

There were African slaves in New Netherland. Some of them "belonged" to the Dutch

West India Company. They unloaded ships, protected the colony against the Indians, and worked on farms. After years of service, the company would give them "half-freedom." That meant they could travel in the colony, marry, and own property. In return, the slave paid the company a yearly tax.

Peter had about 50 slaves working on his farm and in his house. The slave children went to school at his bowery. One of his last acts as governor was to give freedom to eight half-slaves. He also granted them land near his bowery.

Peter had a chapel built on his bowery. He paid a minister to come on Sunday evenings to preach. People sometimes made the trip from New Amsterdam to Peter's bowery to listen to the preacher.

Peter believed there was only one true church and that was the Dutch Reformed Church. It was the church of his father and his grandfather. It was the official religion in the Netherlands.

But even though it was the official religion in Holland, not all people believed in it. There were other churches, known as hidden churches. Their members worshipped secretly. The Dutch government knew about the hidden churches, but it didn't try to stop them as long as they stayed hidden.

When the Dutch West India Company started New Netherland, it said the Dutch Reformed Church would be the official religion in the colony, too. To Peter, that was just fine. But he wasn't as **tolerant** as the Dutch government. He didn't want any hidden churches.

When a group of Jews came to New Netherland in 1654, he asked the Dutch West India Company to let him send them away. The company said no. Sending them away would be bad for business because the company had Jewish stockholders. Peter let the Jews stay, but they had to worship in secret.

In 1657 another religious group called the Society of Friends, or Quakers, came secretly into New Amsterdam. These people were called Quakers because they shook when they felt the spirit of God. When two Quaker women started quaking on the streets of New Amsterdam, a crowd gathered. Peter had the two women arrested and banned from the colony.

A young Quaker man named William Hodgson was with the women. He fled across the river to Long Island. Before long, he began to preach. He was arrested and returned to New Amsterdam.

When he was brought before Peter, the young man didn't take off his hat. He also addressed Peter as if he knew him well. These signs of disrespect made Peter mad. He sentenced the Quaker to hard labor at the fort. But Hodgson would not do the work. He believed he was in jail because he was a Quaker, not because he had done something wrong. He was standing up for what he believed. Peter was furious, and he had the young man whipped with a rope.

Peter tried to forbid religions other than the Dutch Reformed Church, but that didn't work. The Bowne House in Flushing, New York, was built in 1661 by John Bowne, who allowed the Quakers to meet there.

To protest, Quakers in Flushing, New York, came out of hiding. They worshipped in public. Peter had some of them arrested. Their neighbors and friends wrote a letter of protest. It was a strong argument for the basic right of religious freedom. Over 100 years later, religious tolerance was one of the most important ideas put forth in the U.S. Bill of Rights.

When the Dutch West India Company directors heard about Hodgson and the Quakers, they told Peter to stop picking on people of other religions. They ordered him to leave people alone as long as they didn't oppose the government or bother anyone.

The company's reason for being open-minded was selfish. It helped business. But whether the reason was selfish or unselfish, the outcome was good. New Netherland became more tolerant.

The small farms and little homes of New Amsterdam in Peter's time were gradually replaced by the tight grid of streets and the soaring skyscrapers of modern New York City.

Surrender to England

Across the Atlantic Ocean from New Netherland, there was a new king in England. His name was Charles II. In 1664, he gave his brother, the duke of York, all the land that was New Netherland. It didn't matter that Charles didn't own it. It didn't matter to him that it wasn't an English colony. He did it anyway. So now all the duke of York had to do was take it.

Peter had long been worried about the safety of the colony. Fort Amsterdam had little ammunition. Time after time he had asked the Dutch West India Company to send more, but the company didn't send it.

Peter had heard that English ships were on their

way to take New Netherland. He sent a letter to the company and asked if it was true. The company told him it wasn't. But the company was wrong.

In August 1664 Peter heard that four English warships were at New Amsterdam. The commander of the ships was Colonel Richard Nicolls. About 400 soldiers were with him. Fort Amsterdam was outnumbered. It had only about 120 soldiers and 20 small cannons.

Peter sent a message to Commander Nicolls. He asked what the ships were doing there.

Colonel Nicolls sent a message back to Peter. It demanded that he surrender New Netherland to the English. The citizens of New Amsterdam heard about the letter, and they talked among themselves about what to do.

Colonel Nicolls sent another letter. Peter and the two mayors of New Amsterdam read it together. The mayors were ready to read the letter to the other citizens. But Peter was angry. He stood up, grabbed the letter, and tore it in half. Then he stormed out.

When England sent a message ordering the
Dutch to surrender New Netherland, Peter was
so furious he tore up the letter.

The mayors told the citizens about the letter. They wanted to see the letter, but it was in pieces. People gathered outside the state house, and Peter had to put the letter together again.

In the letter Colonel Nicolls promised that the citizens of New Netherland would be treated well. They wouldn't be treated like enemies. They wouldn't be killed or taken prisoner. They could keep their land.

The letter gave Fort Amsterdam 48 hours to surrender. Guns were already pointed at the city.

But Peter was ready to fight for New Netherland. It was his job. He asked the soldiers in the fort if they wanted to fight. They said they were ready. He tried to get the citizens in a fighting mood. He spoke to them about the colony and about loyalty.

But the people didn't feel loyal to the Dutch West India Company, and they didn't feel loyal to the headstrong Peter Stuyvesant. He couldn't get them interested in fighting to save New

Netherland. They would rather be an English colony than risk being killed.

The people brought Peter a **petition**. The petition asked him to surrender New Netherland. The mayors, the aldermen, and the sheriff had signed it. In all, 93 citizens had put their names on it.

Peter looked at the list, and his heart fell. His own son, Balthazar, by then 17, had signed the petition. His own son wanted to give up. The minister of the Dutch Reformed Church wanted Peter to surrender, too.

Peter said, "I had rather be carried to my grave." But on September 8, 1664, he signed the surrender. Perhaps his son's name on the petition helped him decide what to do. Peter also knew that the fort could not stand up long against the English. There was not enough ammunition or food.

He led his soldiers out of the fort. Drums rolled, and the English soldiers marched in and raised their own flag. Soon after this, the

Peter hated the idea of surrendering the colony to the English, but he realized they didn't have enough food or ammunition to win the battle.

name of the colony was changed to New York.

Peter had given up the Dutch West India Company's colony in America. Now he had to sail back to the Netherlands to face the government. It wanted to know why had he had surrendered the colony. The Dutch West India Company blamed Peter, and it let the Dutch government know.

Peter told them the facts. He said the colony had no hope of winning a war against the English. He said the people weren't behind him. He said the company hadn't sent enough ammunition to defend the colony.

Peter had not always gotten along with the members of the city council of New Amsterdam. But now they sent a letter. It agreed with what he said. It also said Peter had done the right thing by surrendering.

But the Dutch government was no longer listening. It had a war with England to fight.

Peter's heart was no longer in the old country. He loved America. As soon as he could, he

When Peter Stuyvesant arrived at the muddy little village of New Amsterdam, he saw many ways to improve it. But he never guessed that it would someday become New York City, one of the most important cities in the world.

returned. He and Judith lived on their bowery. When Peter died in 1672, Judith had him buried in the small chapel on the farm. Later a church was built on the site. It was called St. Mark's-in-the-Bowery and is still in New York City. A marker was put up that said he was 80 when he died. It was wrong. He was 62 or 63 years old at the time of his death.

Peter Stuyvesant helped shape the history of what was to become the United States of America. But when he first stepped ashore and walked along the muddy streets of the little village of New Amsterdam, he probably never imagined that it would become one of the greatest cities in the world—New York City.

GLOSSARY

aldermen person who makes laws for a town or city

appeal to ask for something

bowery a farm or plantation

brigade a group organized to do a job

burgher citizen

canals manmade waterways

colony an area controlled by a distant country

council a group of people in charge of making decisions

dike a low wall made of earth or rock to hold back water

outhouse a lavatory that is in a building by itself, apart from the rest of the house

palisade a fence made of pointed sticks or logs

petition a written request

representative a person who takes the place of another

stoop porch

surrender to give up

thatch plant stalks used for roofing

tolerant open-minded

treaty a written agreement

tropics an area with a warm and humid climate year-round

West Indies a chain of islands between the Atlantic Ocean and the Caribbean Sea

CHRONOLOGY

1610 or **1611** Peter Stuyvesant is born in the Netherlands.

1621 Dutch West India Company is formed.

1624 New Netherland is founded.

1626 The Dutch buy Manhattan Island from Native Americans.

1643 Stuyvesant is sent to Curaçao in the West Indies.

1644 Wounded in battle at St. Martin, Stuyvesant must have his leg removed.

1645 Stuyvesant marries Judith Bayard.

1646 Stuyvesant becomes governor of New Netherland.

1647 Stuyvesant arrives in New Amsterdam.

1650 Treaty of Hartford is established between New Netherland and New England.

1651 Stuyvesant builds Fort Casimir.

1653 Stuyvesant appoints city council.

1655 New Sweden surrenders to Stuyvesant; Peach War occurs.

1664 Stuyvesant surrenders New Netherland to the British.

1672 Stuyvesant dies in New York.

COLONIAL TIME LINE

1607 Jamestown, Virginia, is settled by the English.

1620 Pilgrims on the *Mayflower* land at Plymouth, Massachusetts.

1623 The Dutch settle New Netherland, the colony that later becomes New York.

1630 Massachusetts Bay Colony is started.

1634 Maryland is settled as a Roman Catholic colony. Later Maryland becomes a safe place for people with different religious beliefs.

1636 Roger Williams is thrown out of the Massachusetts Bay Colony. He settles Rhode Island, the first colony to give people freedom of religion.

1682 William Penn forms the colony of Pennsylvania.

1688 Pennsylvania Quakers make the first formal protest against slavery.

1692 Trials for witchcraft are held in Salem, Massachusetts.

1712 Slaves revolt in New York. Twenty-one blacks are killed as punishment.

1720 Major smallpox outbreak occurs in Boston. Cotton Mather and some doctors try a new treatment. Many people think the new treatment shouldn't be used.

1754 French and Indian War begins. It ends nine years later.

1761 Benjamin Banneker builds a wooden clock that keeps precise time.

1765 Britain passes the Stamp Act. Violent protests break out in the colonies. The Stamp Act is ended the next year.

1775 The battles of Lexington and Concord begin the American Revolution.

1776 Declaration of Independence is signed.

FURTHER READING

Davis, James E., and Sharryl Davis Hawke. *New York City.* Milwaukee: Raintree, 1990.

Egger-Bovet, Howard, and Marlene Smith-Baranzini. *US Kids History: Book of the American Colonies.* Boston: Little, Brown, 1996.

Fraden, Dennis B. *The New York Colony.* Chicago: Children's Press, 1988.

Siegel, Beatrice. *Fur Trappers and Traders, the Indians, the Pilgrims, and the Beaver.* New York: Walker and Co., 1981.

Spier, Peter. *The Legend of New Amsterdam.* Garden City, N.Y.: Doubleday, 1979.

Spier, Peter. *Of Dikes and Windmills.* New York: Doubleday, 1969.

Warner, John F. *Colonial American Home Life.* New York: Franklin Watts, 1993.

INDEX

INDEX

PICTURE CREDITS

ABOUT THE AUTHORS

JOAN BANKS remembers being fascinated by Peter Stuyvesant in fifth grade. A former librarian, she has written more than 100 books and articles, for both children and adults. She has a bachelor's degree in journalism from the University of New Mexico and a master's degree in library science from North Texas University. A native of Tulsa, Oklahoma, she now lives on 13 acres near Joplin, Missouri, with her husband, three cats, a dog, and four geese.

Senior Consulting Editor **ARTHUR M. SCHLESINGER, JR.** is the leading American historian of our time. He won the Pulitzer Prize for his book *The Age of Jackson* (1945) and again for *A Thousand Days* (1965). This chronicle of the Kennedy Administration also won a National Book Award. He has written many other books including a multi-volume series, *The Age of Roosevelt*. Professor Schlesinger is the Albert Schweitzer Professor of the Humanities at the City University of New York, and has been involved in several other Chelsea House projects, including the REVOLUTIONARY WAR LEADERS biographies on the most prominent figures of early American history.